Ministry with Black Single Adults

Sheron C. Patterson

Wanda,
Keep the faith!
Sheron
Patt
Dec. 1, 1993

DISCIPLESHIP RESOURCES
MATERIALS FOR GROWTH IN CHRISTIAN FAITH AND LIFE
P.O. Box 189 • Nashville, TN 37202 • Phone (615) 340-7284

Revised 1991.

Cover art by Claudia Williams.

Unless otherwise indicated, all scripture excerpts are from the Revised Standard Version of the Holy Bible.

Library of Congress Catalog Card No. 90-80746

ISBN 0-88177-087-6

MINISTRY WITH BLACK SINGLE ADULTS. Copyright © 1990 by Discipleship Resources. All rights reserved. Printed in the United States of America. No part of this book may be reproduced in any manner whatsoever without written permission except in the case of brief quotations embodied in critical articles or reviews. For information, address Discipleship Resources Editorial Offices, P. O. Box 840, Nashville, TN 37202.

DR087B

CONTENTS

PREFACE *iv*

1. THE NEED FOR MINISTRY   1

2. WHO ARE BLACK CHRISTIAN SINGLE ADULTS?   14

3. HEALING MALE-FEMALE RELATIONSHIPS   31

4. THE CASE FOR CELIBACY   42

5. STARTING A SINGLE ADULT MINISTRY   47

APPENDIX: SINGLE ADULT SURVEY   56

ENDNOTES   58

FOR FURTHER READING   59

PREFACE

This book would not have been possible without the help and encouragement of a number of people: Dr. Zan W. Holmes, Jr., who permitted me to follow my heart and start a ministry for single adults at St. Luke "Community" United Methodist Church in Dallas, Texas; Dr. Dick Murray, my seminary professor who believed that I could write this book and assisted me in the early stages; my parents, the Covingtons, who taught me to always care about others and to help people whenever possible; my two-year-old son, Robby, who graciously and sometimes not so graciously shared his mommy with the personal computer for several months; and my husband, Robert, who continues to understand that my ministry with single adults is not a passing whim but an unshakable calling from God.

This book is dedicated to the millions of single adults who are striving for self-understanding, self-acceptance, and true happiness. All of this is possible through God.

Chapter One
THE NEED FOR MINISTRY

Being Black, Christian, and Single

To be a Christian single adult who is a Black American is a threefold identity. You are Black, you are seeking to follow Christ, and you are not married. For some, the combination of these three descriptions is a smooth addition of pleasant realities. For others it can be a rough juxtaposition. What different people make of it depends on how they see themselves, their race, their faith, and their single status.

As leaders of ministries to Black single adults, we need to recognize and hold up the rewards and possibilities of being Black, single, and Christian. Black Americans have always been a resourceful people. Turning chitterlings into a delicacy was no small feat. Personal joy and satisfaction can be part of the Black single Christian life, especially when singles understand that singlehood is not a curse, and that marriage does not guarantee happiness. Life for singles can assume a positive tilt when they

- Live for God;
- Seek to know more about God;
- Seize opportunities to help others;
- Go places, rather than sit at home, waiting to be discovered;
- Spend time on self-improvement; and
- Bravely establish a faith in God that affirms their ability to make it in life, just as they are.

This is when life can be positive.

There is, however, another side to the story. Being Black, single, and Christian is not an easy path for a number of reasons. No one can deny, for example, that the Black-American experience has been one of racial oppression and discrimination for generations. Today, skyrocketing out-of-wedlock pregnancies and crippling drug abuse haunt our neighborhoods. Fear of crime imprisons neighbors inside their own homes. We are a people of multi-struggles. And, as a result, we have collective mental and emotional scars, such as self-hate, fear of success, and prejudice against one another due to light or dark skin tones.

In addition, we know that living authentically as a Christian in today's world is difficult at best. The "if it feels good then do it" way of living is the order of the day. Life as a practicing Christian requires determination and hard work if one is to live the faith. Also, being a Christian is choosing to be different from the rest of society. This is because we live in a time when the wrong is often promoted as the right, and the right is ridiculed and relegated to the unpopular. Authentic Christians who stand up and fight for the right will risk being labeled as lame, oddballs, or weird.

Some difficulties arise, furthermore, just from the nature of being single in our society. This is because the single status has built-in problems such as vulnerability, weakened support systems, and few sources of consistent positive affirmation. Being a single person within a group that is experiencing racism, genocide, and more, can subconsciously produce anxiety. But everything is not hopeless.

Despite all the difficulties, the Black single adult who is Christian is the most eligible for successful living in the 1990s and beyond. As it was with our ancestors, so it is with us—our destiny as a people is tied to the church. Before discussing what the church can offer, however, let's look more closely at some of the very real issues and problems that create the need for this ministry.

A Network of Needs

There are a number of factors that call out to us to address the need for ministries with Black single adults. When we look closely at these factors, furthermore, we find that we need to reflect on what "ministry" will entail. Take, for example, the imbalanced male-to-female ratio in the Black population. This reality is well publicized among the Black singles circuit. The 1988 U.S. census figures report that there are 9,603,000 Black men in America and 11,618,000 Black women.[1] These figures prove that there is truth to all the talk. Most important, they validate the ongoing claims of single Black women that "there are no men out there."

Where are the men? A disproportional number are inaccessible. Mounting evidence suggests that a near majority of working age Black men (ages fifteen to forty-four) are alcoholics or drug abusers; or they are in prison, unemployed, infected with the AIDS virus, or suffering from some other life-threatening condition.[2] Such figures lead many in the Black community to understand our Black men as an "endangered species."

This population imbalance taints the Black singles scene with the somber reality that partners are a scarce commodity; marriage or remarriage may not occur. Even dating is infrequent at best. This reality produces a host of reactions ranging from fear to indifference. One purpose of ministry, therefore, might be to help people who are suffering under these conditions to sort out their own feelings, reactions, and responses. What can the Christian faith and the Christian community contribute to those who struggle with these realities? The answers may not be simple. Yet, with God, singles can weather the storms of life, and handle the situations and circumstances that are beyond their control.

A Growing Singles Population

Another statistic that underlines the need for ministry with Black single adults concerns their growing numbers in the total population. It may be surprising to learn that, proportionately, Black singles have outnumbered white single adults for many years. Further, the most recent figures (1988) indicate that there continues to be greater singleness in the Black community. The chart below reveals the relevant data.[3]

CHART 1

Marital Status and Living Arrangements for White and Black Population

	White	Black	
Married, spouse present	58.5	35.1	Percentage of Total Population
Never Married*	24.4	39.4	
Separated	1.8	6.9	
Widowed	7.1	8.3	
Divorced	7.3	9.2	
Other	0.9	1.2	

The number of Black single adults has consistently risen over the last four decades. The latest U.S. Census indicates that there are 4,077,000 never-married (always single) Black men; 538,000 sepa-

---

*Since the term "never-married" suggests marriage as the norm for all singles, I shall be suggesting another term—"always single"—as an alternative. Since the census records refer to "never-married," however, I have retained this reference here. See the discussion of this on pp. 14-15.

rated Black men; 343,000 widowed men; and 814,000 divorced men. Compare these figures with those for Black women: 4,288,000 who have never married; 928,000 separated; 1,415,000 widowed; and 1,140,000 divorced.[4] Once again, the figures are discouraging for many singles, especially those who hope to become married. This is a context in which ministry is needed.

Relationships on the Wane

Another concern in the singles situation is the reality that quality relationships are on the wane (whether they are romantic or platonic ones between men and women, or simply friendships between persons of the same sex). In present-day North America this is due, at least in part, to superficial, materialistic attitudes and behavior that practically block persons from being honest, thoughtful, and considerate of others. Thus, the level of trust is reduced, if not eradicated. Sadly, in place of trust and consideration is a mode of entering relationships with a "what's in this for me?" attitude.

Researchers have documented that trust is disappearing, particularly from male/female relationships. One cause has to do with the plight of Black males. For a variety of reasons, many Black males are chronically unemployed (or underemployed) and this "strains the family relationships to the point that women hold low expectations for realizing a stable monogamous marriage."[5]

There is truth to the research, and the point is not merely "academic." I overheard two women discussing their attitudes toward meeting men. One said to the other, "After I meet him, even if the conversation went well and we seemed to have a lot in common, when he says he'll call at such and such a time and day, I know from experience that he won't. Even when I am in a steady relationship, I usually don't hear from the guy but once or twice a week and then that's good. I've learned not to expect much from them; that way my feelings don't get hurt."

The lack of trust between the sexes has fueled intense animosity and fierce bickering. These smoldering emotions have slowly but surely escalated into a full-scale war of the sexes. The absence of trust and the pressure of competing materialistic values increase the isolation, loneliness, and fragmentation of singles. Backstabbing, jealousy, and gossip are the by-products. Quite apart from the issue of marriage, prospects can seem bleak even for the formation of significant friendships. Can the church bring any word of hope or relief into this situation?

The Problem of "Independence"

Another less talked about, yet potent factor affecting relationships in general among Blacks stems from the civil rights that were gained during the '60s and '70s. Attaining these rights resulted in the softening of racism to some degree. Today Black men and women can move about locally and nationally, with few societal restrictions. We are able to attend virtually any college, choose any field of study, and pursue job offers anywhere. We are no longer simply the downtrodden group of people living under the brutal hand of Jim Crow, forced to the backs of buses, allowed into a handful of dead-end occupations.

The result of this is that many Blacks have prospered individually. We have become what sociologists term "independent economic units" and, sadly, it seems that we don't need each other the way we used to.[6]

As bleak as the past injustices were, their effect was racial cohesion. We cared about each other, because we knew that no one else would. Meeting, dating, and simply gathering with other Blacks was automatic, because we had no place to go other than the Black community.[7]

Now our circumstances are improved and we can (and do) go our separate ways. This freedom, though sweet, has indirectly and unintentionally undermined our patterns of building relationships. Much to our surprise, as integration has become a way of life for many Black Americans, we seemingly have forgotten how to come together. As a result, there are comparatively few places where Black single adults can meet and really talk with each other.

The Need for a Meeting Place

The majority culture commonly finds the workplace a fertile meeting ground. Conversely, the workplace is often where Blacks find themselves the only Black or one of few Blacks scattered throughout an office or plant. In many cities and suburbs, furthermore, Black singles are becoming a mobile group. They find themselves living in areas where they are isolated and secluded from other large groupings of Blacks.[8]

Again, forces of loneliness and isolation seem to rise on all sides. But what are singles to do? What are *Christian* singles to do? Many singles today try to meet other people in places such as bars and nightclubs. However, these smoke-filled, dark atmospheres are no simple solution for those singles who are seeking to be Christians. The Christian single who turns to the club circuit will find, more often than not, that a serious attempt to make friends and meet other people is not likely to occur in this setting.

Another popular means of meeting others is through organizations such as professional groups, college alumni, sorority and fraternity gatherings, and introductions by friends.[9] These surely hold some promise of significant relationships for singles, yet again there will often be issues of competing value systems for those who are Christians. In a culture so fragmented by "independence," where are singles to turn?

For Black singles the church is the time-tested meeting place. The church is an appropriate arena for Christian socialization, building a network of friends, and constructive dating. This is *not* to suggest that the church can or should become the headquarters for a dating service or a social club. Though there are great emotional and statistic pressures in our society, the role of ministry with singles cannot simply be to try to get everyone married. The statistics show that this is not possible for everyone; nor is it desirable for everyone. Still, traditionally, the church is where nice girls meet nice guys, where friendships are made, and where singles of every calling find their place in a community of relationships with others.

With God, singles can weather life's challenges. Singles ministries can be models of the way we ought to treat each other, by helping persons come together, befriend, trust, and love each other. From this standpoint, the single's relationship with God is uppermost.

What Is Ministry?

In subsequent chapters, we shall discuss in greater detail a variety of situations in which singles find themselves today. In the "real" world, people are single for many different reasons. In one sense, whatever the nature of the situation, these reasons are simply to be understood— not questioned, challenged, or, necessarily, even changed. Yet, when we speak of ministry, we are also speaking of something that always looks beyond what *is* to what *can be*. What does it mean in the Christian community to be in *ministry* with Black single adults?

Living positively as a Christian single who is Black means, above all, having a strong faith in Jesus Christ as Lord and Savior. In order to own such a faith, singles need to know Jesus personally so that they can honestly place their lives in his hands. A perfunctory faith, maintained solely because mama and grandmama did it, will not do. Otherwise, the negatives of life may overwhelm.

What is the message of Christ for the church and for singles today? The most fundamental yet revolutionary message that Jesus came to offer is the good news that God loves and accepts each of us just where we are, *and* promises to bring us to wholeness in the kingdom of God. This message really has two parts.

First, God loves and accepts us right where we are. This is the message of creation, acceptance, and forgiveness in Christ. This is what it means to know Jesus Christ as Savior. God loves singles too. God loves them whether they are brown-skinned, have wide noses or tight curly hair, whether they have a boyfriend or girlfriend or not. This seems so obvious yet, in a very real way, it is the true foundation for ministry with singles—a foundation that must not be taken for granted. Singles need to hear the good news that God created them individually, as complete, well-designed persons.

In the light of God's love, a single person is *already whole*. Of course, this is true, at least potentially, for all people. But the affirmation needs to be made here precisely because there are so many pressures on singles in our society. As those charged with creating ministries with Black single adults, we need to be able to affirm the liberating news that singleness in itself is not a curse. Nor does marriage validate or justify one's life. Whether one is single by choice or by circumstance, the good news of God's grace and love already applies in full to the life of every single person.

The second part of Jesus' message, then, concerns the promise of wholeness for all in the kingdom of God. In Jesus' vocabulary, the word *kingdom* meant "rule" or "reign." The kingdom of God exists wherever (and to the extent that) people have discovered the freedom of hearing and obeying God's rule or reign in their lives. This is what it means to know Christ as Lord. Singles may be called to remain single or they may be called to become married. In any case, a deep and growing faith in the love and promise of God can help singles overcome that excessive worry about marriage which far too often takes all the joy out of life.

Moreover, singles ministries should give people strength to say no to self-destructive temptations by teaching them to put God first and not to worry about the rest. If God looks out for the sparrows, surely single adults are included too. Singles ministries cannot determine the will of God for specific individuals but they can encourage people to place God at the center of their lives and, thus, to take courage from the Lord. (A good example of such courage is found in Psalm 27.)

In practical terms, what does this say about the nature of ministry with single adults? For one thing, ministry should help singles find the true freedom of their singleness. What sense does it make for singles to sit around waiting to be married? Where genuine ministry takes place, certain notions will simply have to be challenged. The image of the gallant knight riding up on a horse, for example, began and ended with fairytale books. I knew a woman who hungered so after marriage that she subscribed to all of the bridal magazines, and had already selected her wedding gown and china pattern. She had everything for the wedding except the groom. Her fixation on marriage nearly drove her insane. She did not understand that there was a way to live as a single and to be happy.

Singles have probably heard all of this before. The talk about God's promises and God's love, though true, can seem impotent if the singles are frustrated and angry about their situations as single persons.

Speaking of Priorities

"Forget the Bible, just give me a man," one highly agitated sister demanded at a singles Bible study one evening. Luckily I was able to talk privately with her, to calm her down, and to help her see the liberty of giving her first allegiance to God, not to romance. This can be a hard pill to swallow, but Christianity is about getting our priorities straight.

Speaking of priorities, the Apostle Paul had his in an unbending line. I often look to him when discussing singleness, because he shared his viewpoints on the single life so candidly and poignantly. I believe he was right when he taught that singleness could free one for "undistracted devotion to God" (1 Cor. 7:35). He reasoned that unmarried persons could concentrate on things that pleased God rather than be preoccupied meeting the needs of a spouse.

You may have already discovered that there are some people who have a strong preference for remaining single their entire lives. Maybe they are like Paul who possessed a "gift from God" and was thus enabled to live happily without bitterness or resentment over the absence of a romantic relationship (1 Cor. 7:7). Specifically, Paul's gift was that of focusing his mind on nothing but God.

On the other hand, Paul advised those persons without his intense self-control and singlemindedness to marry rather than to "burn" (1 Cor. 7:9). Whether Paul meant burning in the eternal fires of hell as a result of the sin of fornication, or burning with desire for sexual relations, the man has a timeless point. Singleness carries with it a responsibility and accountability.

For those who hope to be helpful to others through the outreach and sharing of a singles ministry, there is a lot of "sorting out" that has to be done. If the church is not a dating service, is it then a monastery or a convent? How can a singles ministry take seriously both the realities of single existence and all the possibilities of Christian calling?

Getting Down to Cases

Ministry with individual singles in the Christian community can move in a number of directions. Much depends on the particular situation and calling of the individual. Though much of the effort of "sorting out" must wait until the more detailed discussions of subsequent chapters, a few examples at this point will help to keep our discussion concrete.

Take, for example, the case of Sean. At the age of forty-one, he is proud of the fact that he has "never been captured." He plans to remain single forever, and his life sways between the pleasures of "marriage" and the freedom of bachelorhood. When he wants to be alone and experience autonomy and freedom, he does so easily. When he wants companionship and sexual intimacy, on the other hand, he also has no difficulty in accomplishing this. Surely this is not the kind of single life Paul had in mind for persons who opt to remain single always.

Another example is that of cohabitation. Many singles in our culture feel the need to live out the slogan "try it before you buy it." Arrangements for living together or cohabitation continue to increase. Such relationships remain popular due to the low degree of commitment involved. Recent studies reveal that "cohabitation has become a predictable part of the American life cycle, filling intervals before marriage and after divorce."[10] So predictable is cohabitation that it is even found among single adults in the church.

Yet another example is the popular though undisciplined lifestyle of producing and rearing children minus the benefit of marriage. Most prevalent among teens and young adults, over 750,000 families with children are headed by a Black female where the female is under 30.[11]

These examples suggest some very "negative" reasons for choosing to remain single. Such reasons often seem to be based on selfish concerns, and may even involve an intense disregard for the well-being of others. In some cases the results are crippling Black America. These kinds of factors impede the progress and achievements possible as a racial group.

A very different case is that of persons who choose singleness out of a sense of fear or defensiveness. Some who cling to singleness do so because they have little confidence in relationships. Others claim a disinterest in marriage because they secretly fear that they may never marry. Rather than risk hoping and never receiving, they deny marriage and close that avenue of thought.

Yet on a very basic level, all of the persons described above are like everyone else. They all want to be loved. It is natural to want to love and to be loved. The desire to settle down and to raise a family is also something that most people want. All of this is fully in keeping, furthermore, with the biblical story of the way God created the world. In that story, the first humans, Adam and Eve, were joined together in the garden of Eden soon after they were formed. God brought them together and they became "one flesh" (Genesis 2:25). On this basis, the Christian tradition has long taught that men and women in general were designed to be paired into the lasting, trusting, wholesome relationship called marriage.

Still, when we come to the question of marriage, we also find a variety of reasons why people either seek, or want to avoid, this relationship. For one thing, although marriage is great, it can become a source of disrespect and reproach for singles. Our society has a way of penalizing persons for not being married, and some singles feel pressured to marry. A Christian singles ministry will certainly want to hold up the values of love, trust, and commitment as the true foundation for marriage; but this must never be turned into a presumption that everyone must marry, or that a person cannot be whole apart from marriage.

Thus, in addition, we need to recognize and affirm that there are some "good" reasons for wanting to remain single. Consider, for example, the desire of some to improve themselves by pursuing an education or a particular career. Perhaps we need to learn to speak of "good" and "bad" reasons, or at least of "better" and "worse" ones, not only for seeking marriage, but also for avoiding or postponing it.

The Need for Ministry

None of this, of course, should be used to downplay the anguish many Black singles feel. What can you do, after all, when you are lonely, or when you believe you are called to marriage, but your way is still blocked by giant obstacles? Recalling our discussion of the statistics, above, we must remember that many Black singles postpone marriage not because they want to, but because they feel trapped in a social and economic cycle of poverty, joblessness, and discrimination.

Singles ministries are challenged to respond meaningfully and purposefully to all of these needs, and to many others as well. The task is not impossible. But the church must take singles ministries seriously. What we have described above are *not* simply passing trends or fads. They are the very real needs which call out for the creation of ministries with Black single adults.

Why a Singles Ministry in My Church?

The church is the institution that has always molded the mores and consciousness of the Black community. If ever there was a time that we needed molding, it is now. Singlehood in the Black community is a legitimate lifestyle. Whether one is single by choice or by circumstance, each person deserves support and understanding from the church.

In the Black tradition, moreover, the church has always maintained an emotional, nurturing, and interdependent relationship with its members. As a result, the church is considered to be "home" for many persons. It is the place to come and lay down one's burdens or to share one's joys. It must be a home to the single who is wrestling with doubts about self-worth because he is unmarried. The church must be a source of comfort to the divorcée whose husband has left her, as well as a shoulder to rely on for the widower who is having to start life over.

Droves of single persons left the church in the '70s and '80s, under false assumptions. With the promise of affirmative action, they thought they could make it on their own. Now with education, careers, and other trimmings of success, they realize that something is missing. It is the Lord. As this group, as well as others, returns home, they must be greeted with the same warmth that met the prodigal son. Once they come, what will keep them is a church that not only feeds their souls, but meets their daily needs as Black single adults who are Christian.

If the church is to continue in the role of being home, a singles ministry in some shape or form is a must. Whether this is a group of 100 who schedule weekly activities under the leadership of a singles minister, or a group of five who meet with the pastor occasionally, certain priorities will need to be kept in view.

Singles ministries are intended to do at least five things. First, they provide spiritual guidance for single adults in specialized environments such as single adult Sunday school classes, Bible study groups, workshops, and retreats. As we have discussed above, there is often a lot of loneliness in the single life. This loneliness can lead to desperation. If solitude is to be used for the best, it must be a time to come to grips with what God has planned for our lives.

Second, single adult ministries must affirm this lifestyle as a legitimate way of living, rather than covering it with a badge of shame. Such groups can help to ease the stigmas attached to singleness. These stigmas have, in many instances, kept single persons locked out of positions of leadership within their churches.

Third, singles ministries can lead the way for the church's programming to become more sensitive to the single adult situation. For example, we can begin by raising awareness that all the church members don't have families to bring to family night, and that holidays can be scary and lonely times for some single persons. The pastor's sermons could also raise awareness by offering images and illustrations for single persons as well as married persons and families.

Fourth, singles ministries provide a context for forming healthy and positive relationships with the opposite sex. Whether these relationships lead to marriage, or simply fulfill the real need for positive friendships between brothers and sisters, singles ministries have an important role to play.

Fifth, and in some ways most important, singles ministries can be a place where singles deal realistically and compassionately with their calling as Christians. What does it mean for singles to live out their faith in the daily round of life, work, and relationships? What does it mean to be a living witness to the rule of God in the world? Singles of all ages and stations in life long for a place of honest and open community in which to hammer out their responses to such questions.

I believe the Black church can most effectively minister to single people by simultaneously understanding the reasons for singleness, by affirming and accepting the single status and, most of all, by

The Need for Ministry

inviting singles to become fully active and involved in the church family.

Now that we have discussed a number of basic needs and issues related to ministry with Black single adults, let's look more closely at who Black single adults are. We'll address this topic in Chapter Two.

Chapter Two
WHO ARE BLACK CHRISTIAN SINGLE ADULTS?

My observations of how Black Christian singles fuse their faith into their lives have accumulated over the past seven years. During this time I have observed how the lives of many singles have been enhanced by their association with singles ministries. Part of my own ministry, in fact, has been to present case studies or profiles of various kinds of persons that I have encountered. These profiles are designed to give insight into the problems and the possibilities of the single life. Some of them will make you want to laugh. Others will make you want to cry because they describe real people dealing with real problems—the kinds of problems singles face daily.

In addition, these profiles are not "should be's" or "ought to be's." I learned a long time ago that church people are not the perfect ones. Though they don't always act like it, church people should be the ones who realize that they are sinners and are trying to do something to correct it. Let's look together, then, at some profiles of specific people who are Black Christian single adults. (Many of these profiles are composite descriptions. All names of actual people have been changed in order to respect confidentiality and to protect identity.)

Always-Single Adults

The term *always-single* refers to those persons who have never been married. People do not marry for a variety of reasons—sometimes by choice, sometimes by circumstance. The term *never-married*, however, can imply that marriage is the norm against which all single people ought to measure their choices and circumstances. In keeping with the whole point of view that we are trying to develop in this book, marriage is not the norm for all people. Therefore, I have chosen to use the term *always-single* to designate those persons who, for whatever reason, have always been single.

The always-single population in the Black community is a sector that is growing in size. It is also a group that is aging due to the trend toward delaying or postponing marriage among a large number of persons. Always-single adults are a diverse group. They can be anyone—from a recent college graduate to a middle-aged construction worker to an older adult. Yet, they all have one thing in common—they have not married. The reasons for this are numerous. Here is a look at several always-single adults and their encounters with singles ministry.

A Need for Identity

Julie is twenty-one years old and describes herself as "very happy." She spends most of her time either with a small circle of friends from high school, or at work, or at home with her parents, with whom she lives. Julie hopes this lifestyle can go on indefinitely. Here is the way she describes herself.

"The way I live right now is great," she said. "The best part is that I am never alone. I don't think I could take that. Also, I'm not ready to take care of myself. I've been sheltered by my parents all my life. I don't feel prepared to live on my own, to make decisions, and to be a really responsible person. Even in my relationships with guys, I don't feel like I know what I'm doing. I wish I had more knowledge of who I am and where I'm going. I feel like I don't know myself. Right now, my parents are there, and my friends are there for me. I depend on them all to help me make it."

This composite illustrates the young, happy-go-lucky, always-single adult who needs to begin to take responsibility for her or his own life. A large number of young people seem to refuse to grow up. They choose to cling to habits from high school or college, perhaps due to a fear of responsibility and accountability. I believe that a lack of self-esteem is the primary culprit.

Therefore, it is so important for singles—especially young singles—to become anchored in God. They need to know that they are "somebody" in the eyes of God. Also, they need to understand that the world cannot take this reality away. Perhaps they learned this in Sunday school as a child. No matter—tell them again and again. We as a people receive too few positive strokes.

Getting back to Julie, involvement in the singles ministry encouraged her down the path of maturity and self-discovery in the house of the Lord. (It's best to be formed here rather than by the values and ideas from the secular world.) She gained exposure to a broader range of people within the group. These were people who had been where she was, and who were caring enough to share their insights. She benefitted from generous spirits and was nurtured by a kindred community.

Next, Julie learned that she was called upon to contribute something to the world. She studied biblical women who dared to make a difference. She got involved with the singles Black History Month activities and learned a great deal about her identity as a Black American as well. Whether she ever marries or not, Julie is beginning to truly find herself as a Black single Christian adult.

A Need of the Spiritual

Always-single adults can also find themselves at the other end of the spectrum; that is, seeming to have it all, but really having nothing. Take thirty-five-year-old Mike, for example. He has all of the trimmings of success in today's society: a secure job, plush living accommodations, an attractive car and wardrobe. Everything seems to be intact except his perceptions of life and of himself. Mike has chosen to live for his possessions and his money.

When we talked on one occasion, he complained bitterly about "the lack of good women out there." I asked him specifically what he was seeking, and he described a woman more fiction than reality. She had to be perfect, with perfect hair, job, face, body, and so on. I asked where he planned to find such a woman. He confessed that she was only in his dreams. Mike went on to share that he did not really know what he was looking for, because he did not really know himself.

It became apparent that Mike had buried himself under the trappings of success. The search for the perfect woman was actually a way of hiding his personal voids. Becoming a member of the singles ministry helped Mike in several ways. First of all, he came to know God. As a result, he also began to know himself more truly and fully through God. Mike added intentional spirituality to his life. He joined a weekly Bible study. He learned to pray and meditate daily.

As a result, Mike himself says that his life is headed in a new direction. He sees his possessions from a new perspective. They are no longer his gods. They are merely possessions. He feels that his life is now truly under God's direction. Also, he is working on valuing women for who they are inside rather than for what they are or seem to be on the outside only. Again, whether Mike stays single, or eventually decides to marry, he has found a new possibility of friendship.

I Want to Be Married Now

Another side to the always-single lifestyle is the strong, often overwhelming, desire for marriage. In women particularly, the biological clock begins to tick. Some fear that they will not marry until after their fertility is diminished. The desire to settle down and have children is completely natural in many if not most women. Our society's emphasis on fun, however, coupled with the desire for maximum freedom, can make this desire look drab and boring by comparison. As a result, some women struggle with mixed emotions. On one side, they have some desire for marriage. On the other, they want to suppress this desire and to project a cavalier attitude, lest they give off signals that they have the dreaded "want to be married" disease.

The need to be married in always-single persons can become a driving compulsion. It can cause them to feel forced to choose between Christianity and their desire for a spouse. A strong singles ministry can help people work through such doubt, however, and see that they are capable of finding happiness whether they marry or not.

Put God on the Back Burner

Let me introduce you to a person I have met in counseling more than once. She is a thirty-five-year-old always-single woman. I'll call her Carol. Her desire for a husband and children caused her to leave her church and to put God on the back burner for a while.

"I wanted to be married so bad, that I went to what I thought were the right places," admitted Carol. "I made myself available to as many men as possible. I even tried living with guys. I was involved in two trial marriages over a period of five years," she recalled. "But I was fooling myself. I didn't have respect for myself and neither did either of the guys.

"I knew that what I was doing to get a man was not compatible with my faith. I went to church, but not to my church. My church is one where I know the pastor brings the message on home to where you live. I went to safe churches where the message was vague and detached from the real world. I knew I was doing wrong. One day, in the shower, the truth came down on me. I asked God to take away the frustration I was experiencing as I tried to catch a man the worldly way. I put my head under the water, and when I came up, I felt freed and encouraged. I felt like I had a renewed spirit. I realize now that I may never get married," Carol added. "Singlehood is not what I want, but I am ready to accept it."

Carol's attitude is a realistic and a brave one. Most of all, she has mastered the ability to lean on the Lord and to begin to look at other options for her life. No, she has not given up the idea of becoming married some day, but she has allowed the focus on God to become primary in her life. Most of all, she is committed to God to the point that she can say, "Lord, not my will but thine." This is a pivotal step in living life as a happy single person. The alternative is unhappiness and a life that is self-guided.

Men in the Marriage Frenzy

The intense desire to marry is not found solely among women. Take Kenny, for example. Kenny was an incredibly shy young man. He was twenty-seven years old when I met him. One evening before a singles Bible study, he shared with me how he longed to marry. Kenny thought marriage was some type of magical cure for the ills of life. He thought it was the only thing he could do with his life. He saw no other options for self-fulfillment. Kenny also wanted to marry to prove to his relatives that he was capable of sustaining a relationship with a woman, and that he was not gay.

All of Kenny's reasons were unsound. Most were downright wrong. A wife would not automatically erase his woes. It is crucial for leaders of singles to be able to remind people like Kenny that life holds other possibilities. Like guidance counselors holding up a number of possible professions, we need to help singles see that all does not depend on only one option. We all have choices.

In addition, singles ministries can serve people like Kenny by helping them discover that they are not the only ones in their situations. Something new begins to happen when singles are enabled to build a network of female and male friends and, thus, to hold on to the understanding that, despite the hardships, God loves them, too.

A Special Friendship Formed

Let's look for a moment at a very positive example. As a result of shared struggle and common vision, singles can become a great source of strength to one another. In one case that I know of, a few of the older always-single women in the ministry have formed a special friendship. They see their singleness as an opportunity to do positive things with their lives. There is time to help with tutorials at the local elementary school, and to be part of the Big Sister organization. As a group they plan weekend outings together. They also read the same novel in a book-of-the-week plan. One member of their circle has recently adopted a three-year-old daughter. Adoption is a viable means for single people to become parents and to share their love.

Who Are Black Christian Single Adults?

I applaud and encourage this style of productive coping with life's difficulties. These sisters realize that, at this point in their lives, and for whatever reasons, they have not found the husbands they wanted. They have learned, nevertheless, that life goes on without marriage, and that God can still bless life without the presence of a spouse.

The Calm Side of the Marriage Frenzy

The flip side of the marriage frenzy, by contrast, is an amazingly calm attitude experienced by some Black males. The always-single Black man has some seven million sisters from which to pick. He seemingly has all the options: when, where, how, and most of all, whether or not to form a relationship. Black men know that they have the upper hand in the dating game. In rather predictable fashion, they often demonstrate disinterested attitudes toward marriage. Many postpone thoughts of marriage and spend their energies enhancing themselves, seeking the assurance of maturity and the attainment of manhood.

This is the case, for example, with thirty-two-year-old Brian. A good deal of his time is devoted to his job and to what he calls "growing into manhood." "The single life is great. I enjoy working on me. My involvement at church has greatly increased my spirituality and I feel that my life has taken off," he said. "I am developing my faith, and honing my mental skills in regard to my career to their fullest. Also, there's been no lack of attention from the ladies," he added with a grin. "There are so many of them out there for me to meet."

Brian explained that he is not ready for a committed, monogamous relationship. Rather, he establishes "friendships" with many women. These "friendships" are partly platonic and partly romantic relationships. They permit limited levels of contact and communication between Brian and the various women. Brian has the upper hand in these relationships. He decides when they begin or end and the amount of communication there is between each woman and himself.

Twenty-four-year-old Tony is similarly enjoying the single life. Like Brian, Tony is in the midst of soul searching and personal growth. "I like the freedom," he said. "The freedom from long-term commitment enables me to read, think, work, or whatever I choose to do. For example, this past week at the office was very demanding on me. I would like to have had a special lady to unwind with, to talk to, and to share things with during the weekend. But, quite frankly, I only felt the need to have a special lady those two days. The desire to maintain a relationship is more of a fleeting urge that comes and goes. It is not something that I think about all the time.

"Now is a time in my life to grow," Tony continued. "I am turning a major corner in my life. I am finally out of college. I'm done with graduate school, and I've completed the training program at work. I am on my own. I've not really had a chance to grow up and take responsibilities. I'm buying groceries and paying rent for the first time in my life. I need to get this routine down well before I can bring anyone else into my life. Most of all I am not ready to invest in a relationship. It requires a lot of time and energy that I am not willing to give. Plus, I'm a bit spoiled. I have my own likes and dislikes," he said.

Both of these men are fairly active within a singles ministry. They attend most of the events. But they leave soon after the events conclude, forsaking any conversations that might arise afterward, lest a woman get any ideas about latching onto them.

On the one hand, the strong need for self-improvement felt by the two men is commendable and encouraging. Always-single Black men such as these have the time to fill voids in the community as role models and participants in community-based programs such as the Coalition of 100 Black Men, Just Say No to Drugs, and the Rites of Passage programs. Their eligibility—and the numerous women attracted to them—undoubtedly raises their self-esteem. To some degree, this can be positive. Our Black men need to feel good about themselves.

On the other hand, however, what one does with one's eligibility is crucial—especially, what the Christian does with his or her eligibility. Eligibility means promise, potential. It means that one has something to offer. In one sense Jesus was eligible. He had a lot to give to the world, and he gave it all. But singleness and eligibility can also be abused. Rather than being accessible to others, one can use one's eligibility as a power over others. They say a person who is all wrapped up in him or herself is the smallest person in the world. Given the current situation among Black singles, this can be an especially important insight for the men.

At the same time, Black women need to recognize that they live in an era when many eligible men are simply not interested in marriage. The fact is, for many Black women, marriage may not be a possibility. At such a time, however, the hungry-eyed-for-marriage look needs to be replaced with something else, namely, with a sense of confidence that one can live happily and fruitfully as a single person.

Ministry to always-single persons should include helping singles to trust that God has a plan for their lives. This naturally implies broadening the scope of vision to see other options besides marriage. At the same time, this can help singles learn how to reach beyond themselves, establishing other positive relationships that don't hinge simply on marriage.

Divorced Singles

People who have suffered through divorce comprise another group of singles that we need to consider. Though biblically endorsed, the institution of marriage has undergone considerable stress in modern American society. The 1980s was an especially bleak decade for marriages. In this period, approximately one out of every two marriages ended in divorce.[1] In the Black community particularly, the institution of marriage has been in great trouble. In the 1960s there were sixty-two divorced Black persons in every 1,000. In 1988 that figure jumped to 263 per 1,000 persons.[2] Also it should be noted that these figures greatly surpass rates for the Anglo and Hispanic communities.

Divorce has not been adequately addressed or understood in the Black community, even though the numbers have been skyrocketing. Divorce is a taboo subject in many Black churches. This seems to reflect an attitude that "if we ignore it, maybe it will go away." We know that divorce is occurring. We can even figure out some of the reasons why. But we don't want to talk about it, or to deal with the victims. As a result, divorcees often suffer silently.

Emotions of divorced persons run the gamut from despair to shame, from a sense of incompetence (at the inability to keep the marriage together) to a sense of joy and relief at the ending of an unsuccessful and destructive relationship. Persons experiencing these emotions may best be served if they can vent their feelings in a positive, supportive environment such as the church—an environment where they know that they are loved no matter what, a place where they know that their relationship with God has no end. Also, they may often need help in affirming that the failure of their marriages does not mean that they have failed as persons in life. Singles ministry can and should be a means of helping them to begin again.

As leaders of prospective leaders, we need to be especially alerted to the fact that ministry with this group may need to be more aggressive. Our society has not unanimously agreed that the church is the place to find relief. Recreational drugs, workaholism, and mental escapism also compete. As a result, general church programs need to be supplemented with more direct forms of ministry. Don't misunderstand, God is truly a waymaker; but one of God's ways comes in the form of church-sponsored programs—for example, individual counseling, group divorce counseling, and small sharing or support groups. Here's what can happen when there is no singles program at the church.

I Needed a Safety Net

Robert had looked drained for the past few weeks. Gone were his outgoing manner and his constant smile. Also gone was his wife of nineteen years. The two were in the midst of a painful divorce. Robert's life was unraveling before his eyes. What he said he needed most was a safety net.

"If only there had been a support group at my church—just a gathering of people who had been where I was—I could have healed a lot faster," said Robert. "Of course, my pastor was there for me with counseling and prayers, but I needed more than that. The ongoing spiritual growth events at church, such as Bible study and prayer meetings, were not enough for me at this crucial time in my life. I needed some specific help because I felt stained with the guilt of being a divorced Christian. I felt that my sin was that I chose not to stop and repair the marriage before it went down the tubes. I could have worked harder to lessen its destruction, but I did not. I wanted out. Rather than subject my children to the trauma of an unhappy marriage, I got out."

Robert could have used a singles ministry during his painful divorce, as he himself recognized. His terminology is accurate; he could have "used" such a ministry in the process of healing. His example illustrates a tangible, hands-on reason why singles groups are needed. Such groups can touch the lives of people who may not be touched in any other way by the church.

What Is Wrong with Me?

Divorce took another direction in the life of Joan. Joan is a thirty-nine-year-old single parent who has been divorced for eleven years. When she agreed to do this interview, she warned me that we would need tissues to wipe our tears. Joan was right. We cried together on this one.

"Singleness has not been pleasant at all for me. I married the wrong man to start with and it's been downhill ever since," Joan said. "During the years after the divorce I always felt unsatisfied with myself and my choice of men. I couldn't develop long-lasting relationships. In the past five years I have not had a date at all."

"How do you handle this?" I asked.

She replied, "I work a lot. I sew a lot. And I go out and do things by myself or with my son." As a last resort to meet men, Joan says she goes to nightclubs. "But the club scene is not enjoyable, because either there are men who approach me with a bunch of lies, or I get no attention at all the whole evening. I must be doing something wrong. I dress nicely and carry myself well, but I feel like I am not pleasing or pleasant. What is wrong with me?"

Divorce had shattered Joan's self-esteem, her perception of herself. She considers herself a failure and, therefore, unlovable by the men she meets. She even feels unlovable by her own son. Despite her woes, Joan remains active in a group and continues to display an unwavering faith. "I have an assurance that, whatever happens, I should be prayerful. My needs are covered. I am prospering on my job. I've never had so much money. I'm healthy and feeling physically fit. But my desire is for marriage. And I've come to understand that God supplies needs."

Joan needed to rid herself of the negative feelings that had accumulated as a result of her divorce. These feelings were like heavy emotional baggage that kept her tied down to the ground. I wanted to help her begin again. She had an ability to soar, but Joan's psychological predicament was too complex for me to handle. I referred her to a local Christian counselor for more intense help. In this connection, it is important to realize that occasionally you will encounter situations related to singleness that are too intricate to address simply by association with a specialized ministry. If intensified psychological help is needed, this must be pursued.

The Unfaithful Spouse

Another problem that some divorced singles have to deal with is that of having been (or having been the victim of) an unfaithful spouse. At thirty-seven, Carlos says he is not the same man he was five years ago, at the time of his divorce. Today he is able to admit that his infidelity was the reason for the divorce. He can also admit that his attitude toward women at the time, and for years after, was the cause of many disastrous relationships. But things have changed for Carlos.

"Today my life is brand new, thanks to God, and to a singles ministry that was able to put up with me. I am a different man and I am thankful. I saw women as objects," Carlos told me, "and I had no respect for them. I was all about getting what I could from them and dumping them soon after. I know I treated my ex-wife like an old shoe. She deserved so much more than that. I lied to her. I flagrantly cheated on her. I was not the loving, supportive spouse I pledged to her and to God that I would be on the day of our wedding. I know also that our children suffered from my misdeeds. I pray that my sons don't grow up to be like I was.

"If it had not been for the church and the singles ministry, I don't know what I'd be like today," Carlos admitted. "I was running the wrong way fast. For some reason the other singles in the group took me in. They didn't criticize me or hassle me. They accepted me. At first I had no confidence in the Bible study time. I just went to be going. But after a while, I started to feel like God was speaking to me through the scriptures. I felt like God was calling my name. That let me know that, even though I had been an awful person to my family and to God, I was still forgiven. That meant a lot. Most of all, it meant that I could try again. The dirty slate of my life had been wiped clean and I could try to live right."

For Carlos, the singles ministry was a place of rehabilitation that he might not have received anywhere else. Where else can you find unconditional acceptance, support, and guidance except within the family of God? Such an atmosphere enabled him to begin again with life.

The Compulsive Partner

Marriage was just a game for Kimberly. At thirty-three years old, she had been divorced three times. She was quite bitter about men, God, and the world, when she came into the singles ministry. "I just don't understand why everything always messes up in my life," she said. "Each of my marriages ended because I was no longer happy with the guy. I thought I knew them well enough before we married, but they turned out to be very different after we were married for a while."

After talking with Kimberly extensively, I came to understand that she had never invested enough time in the relationships with her former husbands. After a few dates, she felt she knew them well enough to marry. She and all of her former spouses would have benefited from workshops on premarital counseling and nurturing relationships. Kimberly's unrealistic attitudes were hard to change. She resisted much of what she encountered in Bible study and in the general attitudes of other Christian singles around her. She remained on the periphery of the group for a while, and eventually dropped out. Kimberly's case is a reminder that not all persons can be helped by a singles ministry.

As you can see from the profiles given above, ministry with divorced singles can be very challenging. This is due to a variety of factors, including the range of circumstances and the deep-seated emotions which often characterize this group. Leaders will need to be perceptive and alert to these factors. Leaders will also need to convey a nonjudgmental atmosphere within the group, so that divorced persons will feel comfortable. Like always-single persons, divorced persons often feel an emptiness because they are without a spouse. Unlike always-single persons, divorced persons once had spouses that they subsequently lost. As such, one of their primary needs is to become free of the negative memories or behaviors of their former marriages. They need freedom to begin again.

Separated Singles

In some ways, a separated person is in one of the most difficult positions of all. Separated people are often in a no-win situation when it comes to membership in a single adult ministry. Some singles groups welcome those who are separated on the basis that a single adult is a single adult. Some do not offer such a welcome because a separated person is not legally an unmarried adult. It is important to note, furthermore, that being separated is a status that many single Blacks experience due to the fact that such a high number of marriages end in divorce.

Regardless of its causes, separation can be a time when persons need guidance and support from a singles ministry. If the separated person's motives are pure, that person should be permitted into the group.

Forty-five-year-old Andy was separated. He came to the singles ministry because he was experiencing a deep inner pain of betrayal. His wife of ten years was having an affair. He confronted her with his knowledge of the affair, and she promised to end it, but had not done so. Andy felt trapped, thinking that the only way out was a divorce.

During the first few months of his separation, I urged him to begin an intense Bible study plan, to immerse himself in the Word of God, and to strengthen his relationship with God, so that he would be shored up for his unpredictable future. After much prayer and fasting, Andy decided he could make a second attempt with his wife. He returned to the marriage, and it is still intact.

Separated Christians present a challenge to singles ministry. They are at a crossroads. To be married or not to be married—that is their question. A singles ministry can be a place of refuge for separated Christians who are confused and in need of guidance or a place to rest and gather their thoughts. Most of all, a singles ministry can be seen as a place to discover options for their lives.

A Battered Wife

Take Cathy, twenty-nine, for example. After nine months of marriage, she found herself a battered wife. Her husband, Terry, began to hit her soon after they were married. "There was never a clue before," she said. "He was gentle, kind, and easygoing." The punches escalated to severe beatings, and she knew she had to get out of the marriage before he went too far and killed her.

Cathy was initially reluctant to come back to the singles group because of the embarrassment. Cathy and Terry had met in the singles group, and everyone thought they were the ideal couple. However, when she returned to the group, her early discomfort quickly was overshadowed by the release, the companionship, the friendship that she found by talking with other singles who had been where she was.

"I was uncertain about whether to stay married or not when I came to the singles group. I just knew I needed some support from people who knew what I was going through. During the marriage, Terry and I had been active in the couples class. I felt like a fifth wheel there now. The singles group was where I gained strength to make my decision, which was to end the marriage. Surprisingly, some of the other women there had been in my shoes before. Being with them was the best thing that ever happened to me."

Widowed Persons

Widowed single adults are another important segment of the singles population. The age range of persons in this group is varied because death knows no age limits. Regardless of age, the needs of this group are large. Obviously, the death of a spouse is a life-shattering process.

Help from a singles group may enable the widowed person to pick up the pieces and to begin again.

Such a ministry is especially vital in the Black community where there may be few other resources for widowed persons or little knowledge of the resources that do exist in the wider community. Also, just the idea of a customized group to address the concerns of widowed persons may make a tremendous difference for many who feel as if they have nowhere to turn.

Be mindful, however, that widowed persons may not be thrilled to be called single adults. These people are involuntarily single. The title "single" reminds them of their loss. Our widowed persons may be served best through a support group or weekly event of their own.

A Grieving Mate

Let's take a look at one widowed person. Gary was forty when his wife was killed in an automobile accident. Two years after her death, he began signaling the importance of her memory by dating other events from the month, the day, and the year that she passed.

"I experienced a complete feeling of loss," he said. "I was confused and kept asking myself, 'Where do I go from here?' Also there was a tremendous anger within me. Later I learned that the anger was part of the grieving process. Another concern revolved around my two children who were ten and four at the time. What type of parent was I going to be for them?

"My faith went through lots of changes. At the hospital, my faith was strong, but it was smashed at her death. I feel blessed to have received tremendous support from the church. The bereavement committee helped me with the funeral plans, and members of the church called just to talk to me and to see how I was doing.

"I see a real place for a single adult ministry in my life right now. It has a lot of appeal. As a single parent you are consumed by your job, your children, and chores that need to be done around the house. You seldom have the time to reflect and to think about yourself. A singles group would provide the needed support because it is a group with which to share. It is the type of external support that can help me to strengthen my family and to grow with my faith," he said.

It's Hard to Let Go

Making the transition from happily married to singleness is awkward and painful for women like Bea. At fifty-eight years of age, most women are looking toward retirement, becoming grandmothers, and settling back to enjoy their golden years. But Bea seemingly refused to go on with life after the death of her husband, Charles, seven years ago. She considered his death as some type of curse against her.

"I put the fact that I am single in the back of my mind, and I pray to God that I can forget it," she said. "Being single is the hardest life to live once you've been married. You see, marriage became a way of life for me; now I have to unlearn it." Perhaps Bea's generation saw singlehood as a pathetic lifestyle. But in today's world, life is what one makes of it.

Although Bea sorely misses her husband and the married life, she has no interest in dating, believing that dating is "a conflict with her faith." "I would feel like my soul is in great danger," Bea explained.

Single adult ministries are not in the practice of twisting people's arms to get them to see a certain point of view, but we are obligated to free persons from antiquated religious misinformation. Bea's belief that dating is sin was totally unfounded. Perhaps she was operating under assumptions she had carried with her through the years. Luckily, there are many types of dating. Some types are clean, respectable, and fun. I told her this, and I also encouraged her to enjoy life to its fullest.

As with the previously discussed categories of singleness, a singles ministry should try to point widowed singles to new options for life and new ways of thinking of themselves. Widowed singles also need to see themselves as persons with real possibilities, on the threshold of new beginnings.

This may be painful for widowed singles. They may not want to think of themselves without their spouses. The grief process and individual periods of bereavement vary from person to person. Because of this grief variable, it is important for ministries to be sensitive, to take cues from the widowed persons themselves, and not to move too fast or too aggressively. Still, there may be times when a support group of single persons is just what recently widowed persons need, though they cannot voice this need. The pace and approach to such persons must be guided with prayer and meditation.

Singlehood and Black Older Adults

As our discussion of single people moves upward in age range, it is important to examine singleness among older Black adults. Our "elderly Black population has been increasing more than twice as fast as the

Who Are Black Christian Single Adults?

overall Black population. Their numbers are expected to be four million by the year 2000."[3]

The ratio between males and females among Black older adults is similar to what we saw earlier among younger Black adults. The following chart identifies the percentages of Black persons sixty-five years old or older and their single or marital status. "Among Blacks aged 60-64, there are 80 men for every 100 women. And as they age the number of men decreases to 50 men for every 100 women at age 85 and above."[4]

CHART 2
Marital Status of Senior Black Adults

	Married	*Widowed*	*Divorced*	*Never-Married*
Men	56.9	22.1	14.7	6.3
Women	25.0	57.7	11.6	5.6

These figures remind us that the older adult single population cannot be written off. Even though they are older, these singles still have strong emotions and needs like any other age group. Thus, a number of things should be borne in mind when considering a ministry to singles of this age group.

1. Testing the level of interest among older adults for a group that caters specifically to them is always a good idea. Sometimes older adults simply do not want this kind of attention.
2. In order to avoid trying to "reinvent the wheel," be sure to investigate already existing programs for older adults that are in your church or community. You may be able to enhance a program that is already established, even if a new program is not needed.
3. Singles of this age group often do not like to be called single adults. This designation has a negative connotation because, during their younger days, the respectable people were married and the disreputable ones were not.

Older Adult Longed for Ministry

I can remember talking with a pastor who had recently received a phone call from a widow whose husband had been buried two weeks before. The widow, whom I'll call Lucille, called to say that she was lonely and wondered if there was a singles ministry for older persons at the church. When the pastor informed her that there was no such group at the church, she asked him to start one! The pastor followed the widow's request and polled the older adults in the church as to their desire for a special ministry to meet their needs. He was given a negative response.

Even though there was not a groundswell of interest, Lucille's concerns were legitimate. She was looking for a group of single people with whom she could enjoy life. She said that she felt out of place with the married couples with whom she and her late husband had spent time. Unfortunately, a singles group for older adults did not materialize at this church, but the pastor was able to refer Lucille to another singles group for older persons at a nearby church.

The lack of interest in a singles ministry at the church brings up another point about Black older adults who are single. Gerontological research tells us that this age group of persons has lived during some of our nation's most cruel days. They have weathered the storms of Jim Crow's inequities and prejudice, the likes of which many of us have never seen. They lived through a period in history that many of us have only read about. They also grew into old age just as racism began to wane. As a result they may not be accustomed to pampering and special treatment. But that is exactly what they deserve.

More than likely, this same group of people made up the backbone of the church for decades. Many a Black church that stands today does so as a result of chicken dinners that were baked and sold by faithful, and now elderly, church members. In a beautiful sense, we *owe* them special treatment.

Now that we have looked in some detail at the range of single adult experience, let's examine some of the ways singles interact with each other. This is the focus of Chapter Three.

Chapter Three
HEALING MALE-FEMALE RELATIONSHIPS

In my years of working with single adult ministries, one issue has always been crucial—male/female relationships. Relationships seem to deteriorate more every year. Today they can be described as cold, fierce, and dangerously divisive. If this area does not receive immediate help and healing, tomorrow's picture could become even bleaker.

The sociologist duo Nathan and Julia Hare illustrated our situation accurately when they wrote:

> If we had to name the most tragic failure of Black people historically in the United States, we'd have to point to the relations between the Black males and Black females. Our confusion, or negligence in this area is both curious and shocking, because the relationships between male and female are the most intimate and basic of all human entanglements and the most crucial for the subjugation of a people.[1]

Often I've led rap sessions on the topic of male/female relationships and, to my dismay, such events predictably turn into heated debates and yelling matches, which pit the men against the women. At one event seventy-five single adults from around the city packed into a church's small fellowship hall. The discussions became so hot due to flaring tempers and accusatory language that, by the end of the event, I noticed that the men had lined up on one side of the room and the women had squared off on the opposite side. I concluded that this unconscious separation was symbolic of the way it really is. Men and women feel separated from each other. Our bickering has driven us away from each other, and now our backs are against the wall.

Let's Call a Truce

The squabbling, name calling, finger pointing, and eyeball rolling among us has gone on long enough. Let's call a truce in the name of the Lord. Let's allow the church to be the neutral ground in this war of the sexes, a place for genuine healing to occur. The church can and should be the place where we lower our guards, feel unthreatened, and calmly talk our way out of this mess.

The challenge to the church in the 1990s and beyond is to get thoroughly into everybody's business. More theologically, this means that the church must effectively minister to the spiritual as well as to the social needs of the individual. This is not a case of the church overstepping its boundaries because, where God is concerned, there are no boundaries in our lives. The churches must help repair the schism in Black male/female relationships. No other institution but the church has the divine authority to do so.

If this call to our churches to become a center for social healing sounds brash, consider the alternatives: influence from popular songs that scream sex, sex, sex; advice from celebrities and athletes, some of whom live lives of shameless abandon; and coaching from television programming, where there is much fun and little responsibility. Only the church can put us back together again.

In order to understand and accept the church as our neutral ground for healing the relationship schism, we need to rediscover the scriptural basis for reconciliation and reunion. Scripture can remind and instruct us on basic human values. I'd like to suggest Matthew 22:37 as a starting point for a biblical approach to singles ministry: "You shall love the Lord your God with all your heart, and with all your soul, and with all your mind. This is the great and first commandment. And a second is like it, You shall love your neighbor as yourself."

These words of Jesus are not very fancy. Nor do they have hidden meaning. Their very simplicity is a witness, however, to our need for them in our community, especially in the area of ministry with singles. Singles can be so far removed from a positive, basic understanding of each other. Foundational elements of community life such as respect for each other, honor, and recognizing simple right and wrong can sound as passé as the terms *colored* and *Negro*.

If ministries could help singles learn to live these words of Christ, the results would be transforming. Living out the words of Jesus in Matthew 22:37 from the single perspective means that singles will be persons with clearly focused lives. Their dealings with one another will be exemplary. They will be authentic, trusting, and most of all responsible for each other.

The words of Jesus from Matthew 22 cut to the heart of our situation and shed a powerful light of hope. This kind of hope—hope in the power and presence of God—can free singles from worry over the "what ifs" of life. Such hope can strengthen singles to live differently and to discover the other options they have. All of us need to get closer to God.

We need more love for each other. And we need more love for ourselves. Let's look at these three areas individually and apply them to the goal of singles ministries to bring healing to male/female relationships.

Love the Lord Your God

What does loving the Lord have to do with healing male/female relationships? To some, these concerns may seem far removed at first. Yet, when one seeks to truly love God, to serve God, and to be led by the will of God, a great many other things can change as well.

It is perhaps not too much of a generalization to say that many Christian singles feel pulled in opposing directions by their emotional, spiritual, physical, and sexual needs. Loving God means being able to say, "Not my will, Lord, but thine." There is a very real freedom that comes with having only one Lord, instead of a number of private or personal "gods" that pull in various directions. By providing a still point in the flurry of vying emotions, the connection with God can bring new perspective into a troubled situation. In the midst of troubled emotions and conflicting advice, where can one turn for wisdom? The Psalmist has said, "The fear of the Lord is the beginning of wisdom" (111:10).

These, of course, are nothing more than basic insights into the ways of Christian spiritual formation and health. The application of these insights is not limited to the lives of singles by any stretch of the imagination. Nor are these insights any more difficult or easy for singles to truly live out. Still, many singles have witnessed to the power of Jesus' commandment in their own lives, and in the kinds of situations that singles face daily. Situations that look hopeless one day can be opened up and transformed—even if only in the smallest of ways at first—by practicing the love of God. As such, loving God and putting God first in life can be a source of freedom, hope, healing, and growth—a source that leaders of Christian singles ministries must not overlook.

Love Your Neighbor

In the second place, Jesus' words call us to love others. In fact, he taught that loving others is one clear evidence and consequence of our love for God. Loving God also means finding balance in human relationships. But what does this mean in the context of male/female relationships? What would it really look like for Black single adults to love each other in this way? And how can this vision be an additional source of healing in the male/female relationships of Black singles?

Let me ask you to engage in an exercise of imagination with me. (You might also try this kind of exercise with a group of singles.) Let's imagine a relationship between a fictional Joe and Jane—two people who have been seriously involved with each other in an exclusive relationship. They've sworn their dedication to each other. Several months into the relationship, Jane decides that she is bored with Joe. Instead of honestly revealing her feelings, she selfishly begins to date other men secretly. What will become of these two? How would you finish the story?

I know how I would finish it, because I have seen cases like this many times. When Joe finds out, he feels betrayed and angry, and vows never to trust women again. He plans to protect his heart by constantly maintaining "women on the side" of his monogamous relationships in the future. This way he can ensure that he won't get hurt.

Jane, on the other hand, has established a pattern of putting her needs before her partner's needs. True love has been shortcircuited by the "me first" approach. This "me first" practice leads to continuous relationship trauma for her, as well as an inability to trust and be trusted in relationships. This is a vicious cycle.

Moreover, the lack of consideration Joe experienced in the relationship with Jane has also weakened if not destroyed his desire for establishing trusting relationships, for months or maybe for years. He may become a calloused participant in the dating world. The women he encounters in the future may be destined to suffer the consequences of his own hardening. And so, the vicious cycle will be extended.

Multiply this scene millions of times, inserting different names and circumstances, and you begin to have a picture of what male/female relationships look like *without* the love of God and neighbor that Jesus was talking about. The point of a picture like this will not be lost on singles themselves. They have struggled with these same dynamics. At some point in their experience, they too will probably encounter a Jane or a Joe. As a consequence, many singles carry with them very negative images and stereotypes of men and women in our community. These stereotypes not only reflect the troubled condition of male/female relationships, they also serve to widen the gulf that presently exists between the sexes.

When asked to describe Black men, most Black women will use the following adjectives: lazy, noncommittal, unfaithful, low self-esteem, trifling, and sex-crazed. When asked to describe Black women, the responses from Black men include aggressive, jealous, materialistic, possessive, domineering, and too independent.

In a nutshell, Black men see Black women as too strong, and Black women see Black men as too weak. Granted, these views are not exclusive to the Black community. They have, however, had a special impact on our relationships. Like the mule wearing blinders as it pulls the plow in the field, we can see only a constricted portion of what is actually before us.

An Exercise in Loving One Another

Let's take off the blinders. Just as our lack of love for one another becomes visible in the stereotypes we have of each other, so the possibility of finding real love for each other can become visible by challenging the stereotypes. I have found that a helpful means of healing stereotypes is to look beyond them and to uncover the reasons that cause us to earn the unflattering labels. This examination of stereotypes is even more effective when it is done in a group setting with both males and females present.

One approach I have used, for example, is to ask the men to list their stereotypes of women. I write these on a chalkboard before the group. Then I allow the women to make the same type of list. After each group has compiled a list, we go down the list and try to figure out why each stereotype was chosen. Then we permit the gender that carries the stereotype to defend it.

For example, some women are labeled as "gold-diggers" because they are constantly looking for a wealthy man. But the women in the group may explain that, in reality, such women are only seeking a secure relationship with a man who is ambitious, goal-oriented, and determined to succeed.

It can be interesting at this point to see how the men will respond. Do they see the real need that lies in back of the gold-digger stereotype? Some may answer that they want to be more determined to succeed in life rather than dwell in hopelessness or live in a dream world of procrastination. The answers will vary, but the point is to enable all to see that the root causes for stereotypes are not necessarily flaws within persons, but needs.

Something similar occurs when women are given a chance to discuss one of the male stereotypes, for example, that Black men are noncommittal. In response, the men may want to explain why some of them do not wish to commit to relationships. Some common answers include fear of rejection, or the fear of an inability to make and keep a Black woman happy. Once again, all may begin to recognize the need that lies in back of the stereotype.

If men and women are permitted to explain and address these kinds of stereotypes, a more hospitable understanding and even a tolerance can develop between the sexes. Most of all, the men and women can begin to see that they are stronger and healthier when they stand together than when they are at odds. They can begin to truly love each other.

The Need for Self-Love

The third part of Jesus' great commandment has to do with the most elusive need of all—the need for self-love. What is self-love? How is such love connected with the problems singles encounter in their relationships? Weren't we just talking about the need to put others first? How can singles do that and love themselves at the same time? Maybe part of the problem has to do with learning what real self-love is.

Self-love has seemed elusive at times in the Black community. For many in the Black community the by-products of racism, such as self-hate and self-degradation, have snuffed out the ability to love one's own person. A now-famous experiment from the 1940s tested Black children's images of themselves. They were shown two identical dolls. The only difference in the dolls was that one was white and the other was black. The researcher asked a group of Black boys and girls to select the doll that was the prettiest, the smartest, and the nicest. Most of the children selected the white doll. This same experiment was conducted again in 1989, and the results were close to the original findings.[2] If we as a people do not love ourselves, but instead feel a sense of worthlessness, certainly our ability to be loving, nurturing friends or mates is hampered. Such feelings of worthlessness will certainly influence the way we behave in relationships.

Destructive Self-Images and Relationships

I contend that an important part of our role as leaders in ministry with singles is to help singles discover new options for their lives. Singles struggle not only with poor images of one another; they also struggle with poor images of themselves. But how can singles find healing in the area of self-image? And how can they connect this healing with the problems they face in male/female relationships?

In keeping with what I have already shown, one approach that I have found helpful is the use of case studies or profiles, that is, accounts that allow singles to identify problems and possibilities for themselves. Such accounts can be humorous. They should be anonymous. They should not identify particular individuals. Even if the profiles are caricatures, however, they must identify real issues. Otherwise they will be of little use in helping singles to find real healing.

The following profiles represent just a few of the typical patterns of poor self-image and dating style that I have observed over the past years. These styles can be found with either gender, and at most any age. If you work among singles, you will be able to think of others. I have intentionally drawn these as caricatures yet, as self-images for male/female relationships, they have a very serious side. They are negative and destructive, resulting from our common inability to love God, each other, and ourselves. In the next section we will look more closely at some of the positive images for male/female relationships offered in the Bible. For now, let's take a sober look at how things often go awry.

The first caricature I will call Limpy Linda. Limpy Linda's weak sense of self is evident in her desire to be completely subservient to the wishes of her potential mate. Because she spends so much time trying to please and know others, she has lost any clear sense of her own unique identity. As a result, she has no self-confidence or any idea that she can be a complete person in her own right. Rather she is waiting for a man to enhance her life. At the same time, Linda has become frustrated and angry from trying to please so many people and never accommodating herself. Linda's life could change, however, if she could only discover the connection between truly knowing and loving herself and being truly known and loved by others.

Another example of the connection between poor self-image and dating style is that of Greedy Greg. Greedy Greg is engaged in a frantic search for a wife. His approach is to arrange as many dates with as many women as possible. But these hasty relationships don't deepen or last because he is going at such a rapid pace. Greg doesn't take time to develop and nurture the relationships. To hear him tell it, Greg has become disenchanted with the opposite sex. He has become more and more disinterested in meeting people or in building relationships. The real culprit in Greg's plight, however, may be his own fear of really meeting himself. After all, in order to grow really close with another person, you must allow yourself to be known.

Loosy Lucy, on the other hand, sleeps around a lot. She does this because it seems glamorous and exciting. Most of the women on her favorite TV programs do the same thing. Physical love is the only kind of love Lucy knows. Lucy also sleeps around due to her very normal desire to be loved. Like many people, she wants to achieve a satisfactory romantic relationship, to choose or to be chosen by a desirable mate. But her method of pursuing this goal is counterproductive. She has put "the cart before the horse." First she beds the men down, and then she wants to talk about a committed relationship with love and fidelity. In the meanwhile, Lucy's reputation before others (both men and women), as well as her own sense of self-esteem, stands in real jeopardy. Her willingness to try to land a man by means of sex is an index of her own bruised self-image. The final irony is that this approach to dating is not likely to bring Lucy any nearer to the kind of relationship she ultimately desires.

Yet another problem emerges in the sketch of Hang-on Harriet. Hang-on Harriet feels that it is better to have someone, anyone, than to have no one. Therefore, Harriet is not selective in her choices of dates. Also, she remains in unproductive relationships even though it is obvious that she would be better off alone. She is not comfortable with the idea of being alone because her self-worth is centered in her ability to have and keep a man. Harriet is vulnerable to hazardous relationships because her own sense of value and identity before God is so poorly developed.

A final destructive self-image for dating relationships is that of Gone-Crazy Craig. Gone-Crazy Craig has allowed the obsession to marry to distract him to the point that his life is falling apart. Seeing everything through his desire to marry, Craig is courting personal disaster. The dangers of becoming a person like this include depression, anxiety, insomnia, fatigue, and an inability to work. Realistically, the options for Craig include having a nervous breakdown, or finding a new center for his life and his relationships in God.

Christian Self-Images and Relationships

Thanks be to God, male/female relationships do not have to be this way at all. If singles can learn to love God, and to love each other as they love themselves, transformation is possible. We still have to ask, however, how to translate the hope for healing relationships into a practical working model. Going beyond the negative stereotypes and the destructive self-images, what practical steps can we recommend—steps that will help singles break the cycle of broken relationships, and discover the freedom of new relationships in Christ?

As a consequence of my experience of leading and consulting with singles ministries, I recommend a four-step approach to the issue of male/female relationships. I call this the model of Christian dating. Christian dating is based on a number of biblical teachings and principles.

On the grandest scale, our capacity to interact with each other as sexual beings is a gift from God. This is basic in the biblical story of creation. In the biblical story, after creating Adam, God looks upon him and says, "It is not good for the man to be alone" (Genesis 2:18, NIV). God then went on to create female. After the creation of male *and* female, God declares creation not only "good," but "very good" (Genesis 1:31). In the New Testament, the Apostle Paul picks up the point of the Genesis story in his celebration of the place of marriage in the Christian life: "For this reason a man will leave his father and mother and be united to his wife, and the two will become one flesh" (Ephesians 5:31; Genesis 2:24, NIV). The Bible portrays the capacity for sexual relationship as part of the wholeness and goodness of creation.

Along with this clear affirmation of sexuality, however, the model of Christian dating does not place sex, or even marriage, at the center of male/female relationships. Marriage is not the only goal of healing relationships between male and female. Singles need to be affirmed in the belief that people can date and form friendships for other than sexual or matrimonial reasons. In the model of Christian dating, one can date others just to get to know them more positively, to be a friend, and to build responsible relationships—with or without the possibility of marriage in mind.

In the Bible, we see many examples of relationships, both good and bad, healing and harmful. Looking at the story of Ruth and Boaz, for example, we see a relationship that is built on simple things like honesty, compassion, and truth. Ruth was a young widow from a foreign country who had come to the land of Israel to care for her aging and bereaved mother-in-law, Naomi. Boaz, a relative of Naomi, was evidently a man of some means, with a generous and sensitive nature. Boaz allowed Ruth to gather food for herself and for Naomi from his fields. As the story unfolds, a relationship of mutual respect develops between Ruth and Boaz. According to the customs of the day, Boaz is finally able to marry Ruth when he agrees before his kinsmen to take responsibility for continuing the family line of her deceased husband.

Outdated customs aside, the bottom line of this story is that relationships between male and female can be based on character, shared values, and mutual respect. Ruth and Boaz took time to get to know each other. They each invested something of substance and character in the relationship. They were honest with each other. Also, the story of Ruth and Boaz shows that we should be free from the cultural impediments that block relating to each other as whole human beings—such as the lightness or darkness of skin, hair texture, occupation, and education.

On the other hand, one of the most disastrous relationships recorded in the Bible is that of Dinah and Shechem (Genesis 34). Dinah was a young woman who seems to have been rather superficial in her judgments. According to the story in Genesis, Dinah wanted to visit the "daughters of the land." She was curious and, in terms of the standards of her day, somewhat reckless for a young single woman. In the course of her visiting, Dinah came to the attention of a young prince by the name of Shechem. The story does not give any indication of a developing relationship between Dinah and Shechem. All we really know is that, prior to asking for her hand in marriage, Shechem raped Dinah. A bloody massacre ensued, as Dinah's family retaliated against Shechem's.

Once again, obsolete customs aside, this story carries a timeless point. The true foundation for strong and lasting relationships between the sexes is not sex in itself, or even marriage per se, but shared values and mutual respect. With these simple biblical stories in mind, then, let's look now at the four basic steps of Christian dating.

1. Look for a friend, not a meal ticket, a sex partner, or a stepping stone for climbing the social or corporate ladder. "A friend loves at all times" (Proverbs 17:17). There is a bumper sticker that reads, "If you are rich, I am single." Beyond the humor in this saying lies the terrible possibility of dating and perhaps even marrying someone who has lots of cash, but who makes you sick. Remember the story of Dinah.

2. Date persons with similar Christian convictions. This way you will not have to defend your faith, or compromise your beliefs, to

impress or to keep a date interested in you. "Do not be mismated with unbelievers. For what partnership have righteousness and iniquity? Or what fellowship has light with darkness?" (2 Corinthians 6:14). Remember Boaz and Ruth.

3. Keep God first in the relationship. One of the great mysteries of all human relationships is that relationships themselves can become stronger when they are not made an end in themselves. This has a special relevance to the relationships of male and female. Attend church together. Pray as a couple. Study the Bible together. All of these activities can be a means of strengthening the individual as well as the relationship in the Word of God. "Commit your work to the Lord, and your plans will be established" (Proverbs 16:3).

4. Maintain high moral standards. Celibacy is a real possibility for single persons. Celibacy is abstention from sexual intercourse. When celibacy is incorporated into relationships, each person is afforded the luxury of getting to know the other on many important levels, such as personality, temperament, and character. Developing a heavy physical attachment in the early stages of a relationship, on the other hand, can cloud and confuse these other basic concerns. "I appeal to you therefore, brethren, by the mercies of God, to present your bodies as a sacrifice, holy and acceptable to God . . ." (Romans 12:1).

These are the basic principles and steps that I recommend to singles with whom I am in ministry. The steps are not fancy, nor are they particularly new. They are based, however, on the solid foundation of biblical wisdom and experience. Therefore, as leaders or potential leaders of ministries with Black single adults, I recommend them to you as well. Add to them as you see fit. In any case, our goal should be to do all we can to encourage healing in the relationships of single men and women in the Black community.

At this point, I want to pick up in a special way the topic of celibacy. The discussion of celibacy is relatively new in the Black community. As I have just suggested, however, the practice of celibacy can be a very important step in the healing and nurture of relationships. Therefore, in the next chapter, we shall look at this practice in more detail.

Chapter Four
THE CASE FOR CELIBACY

I usually save the topic of celibacy until the end of my presentations. I don't want to lose my audience too soon. The topic of celibacy is about as popular as cod liver oil. We know that it is good for us, but no one wants to practice it.

A few years ago I conducted a workshop on the topic of singles ministry in the Black church at a national singles meeting in Nashville. Everything was going great until I raised this issue. Then my workshop went downhill fast. To my amazement, a glaze seemed to cover the eyes of most of the persons in the room. I sensed disinterest and boredom within the formerly lively group. Eventually I began to receive side-long glances, and I heard the sucking of teeth. Then I knew for sure that I had lost them.

As a leader or prospective leader of single adult ministries, O reader, I certainly don't want to lose you at this point in the book. Before I share my thoughts on celibacy, let's look for a moment at what single adults are saying about this topic.

If you have an interest in polls, I took an informal, unscientific survey of 100 single adults. Of that group, seventy-eight were female and twenty-two were male. Seventy-nine were always-single. Twenty were divorced. And one was widowed. I asked this group the following question:

Is celibacy a reality in your life today? The results were surprising. Seventy-two of the singles stated that celibacy was a possible way of life for them. Seventeen stated that it was not. And eleven singles were not able to answer the question.

I have also conducted numerous interviews on this subject as well. What follows is a sampling of what singles are saying and doing with respect to the practice of celibacy.

A Difficult Determination

Katrina, a thirty-five-year-old divorced female, is determined to remain celibate. She shared, however, how this can be a difficult lifestyle to maintain. "Dating has not been working for me. I've been practicing celibacy for seven months and the guys definitely do not like it," she said. "Three or four years ago in the dating scene, the topic of sex did not come up so quickly. Now, on the first date, the guys are asking to come over and stay the night. I usually refuse these initial invitations by reminding my date of the current problems with sexually transmitted diseases. This is my first line of defense," Katrina said with a chuckle. "When they continue to pressure me I tell them the real reason—I'm saving myself for my husband.

"Most of the guys just laugh in my face and I never see them again," she continued. "A few stick around to see if I'm really serious about it. Others try to lecture me about what I'm missing. But that is exactly the point. I know what I'm missing—meaningless sex with a total stranger who wants physical satisfaction that night and nothing more. Chances are, if we saw each other the next day on the street, he'd act like he didn't know me. I've had those types of experiences one too many times."

The Male Side of Celibacy

George, who is twenty-nine years old and has always been single, is striving to be celibate as well. He also confides, however, that this can be an especially difficult choice for a male to follow. One problem is the threat of ridicule and misunderstanding, not only from other men, but from women as well.

"I think marriage is a truly sacred institution," he explained. "Marriage is something that you just do not play around with. Therefore, when it comes to dating, I don't date a person I would not marry. My faith informs all of my dating activity. And as a result, I take dating seriously. I feel that sex is an ultimate expression of who you are. I just don't want to play around with something so important.

"People ask me why I'm not running after all the beautiful women in the singles group," George added. "It seems especially frustrating to the sisters because they've come to expect a man to always hit on them for sex as a sign that he's interested in them. But for me, interest in a woman begins with who she is, not whether I can get her into my bed quickly."

Three Reasons to Consider Celibacy

Having looked at what some singles have to say about celibacy, now it's my turn. I believe that there are three significant reasons why celibacy should be considered.

First, God's gift of sexuality was designed to function within the marriage covenant where there is security, commitment, demonstrated love, and the foundation for the beginnings of a complete family should a child be conceived. If the church could reintroduce and popularize the connection between sex and marriage, the value and importance of marriage, commitment, and responsibility would skyrocket.

Second, the prolific biblical writer, Paul, set forth an important and proven approach to sex, celibacy, and marriage. Moreover, he considered this approach important, not only for himself, but also for the community called in Christ's name. In other words, he advocated celibacy not only because it was conducive to one's own personal health and spiritual maturity, but also because it was of fundamental importance to the witness of the Christian community. Those who follow Christ should uphold the behaviors associated with Christ.[1]

In 1 Corinthians 12:14, Paul wrote that those believers who are filled with the Spirit should use their enthusiasm to "build up the church." I am suggesting that our Christian enthusiasm should be used also to build up the beleaguered Black community. The sex-crazed attitudes that manipulate America have a choke-hold on the Black community. The obsession with the physical is driving us to destructive behavior. Some 60 percent of all Black babies are born out of wedlock. Sexually transmitted diseases are reaching record levels in our community. The practice of celibacy would be one significant way, not only to maintain personal health, but also to contribute to the wholeness of our community as well.

Third, and perhaps most important, sex outside the bonds of marriage is sin. In straight biblical terminology, this is the sin of fornication. The scripture makes crystal clear, furthermore, what we can look for as the outcome of sin. "The wages of sin is death . . ." (Romans 6:23). We might also remember in this connection that in the area of sexual health and identity, "death" can take many forms.

Jesus' Example

When examining the topic of celibacy, I find it helpful to consider the way Jesus handled the issues of sex outside of marriage. One of the most helpful biblical passages illustrating the situation is found in John 4:7-30. Here Jesus had an encounter with an unnamed woman at a water well. The woman came to draw water at a time when no other village women were present. She evidently hoped to avoid being shunned and condemned by others due to the conduct of her personal life.

Jesus looked at the woman and saw her situation and her needs. He began to talk to the woman about religion, yet it was clear to Jesus that she was living two lives. She had one foot in the world, and the other foot in her faith. First Jesus talked with her about the gift of salvation. Then he demonstrated that divine love does not begin or end with "religious" concerns only. Jesus delved into her personal life. He didn't pretend not to see that she was living immorally with a man to whom she was not married. Jesus knew that she'd been married many times and that her life was very confused. With gentle yet clear-headed compassion, he offered her a way out of her painful existence, a new way of thinking about herself. Jesus told her that her life would have to be brought in line with her spiritual commitment.

This parable illustrates that Jesus knows us and is aware of our sins, whatever they may be. Most of all, the story shows us that Jesus forgives, points us in the correct way to go, and calls us to follow.

Keeping the experience of sexual intercourse for the bonds of marriage is yet another means of using the options presented to singles via their faith in God. Abstaining from sexual intercourse outside the marriage bond is a matter of spiritual, emotional, and relational health and obedience. So what if sexual activity among single people is popular in society? As Christians we need to remember that, just because something happens, or is popular, this does not make it necessarily right with God or good for us.

Recalling some of our discussion in previous chapters, we should repeat at this point that there are "better" and "worse" reasons for choosing celibacy. Those who lead in ministries will need to help singles continue to sort out the motives that so often get entangled in the decision to seek or to avoid marriage. Ultimately, the reasons for choosing celibacy must be grounded in the Lord, not in a lack of potential sexual partners, or in anger with the opposite sex, or in the attempt to make oneself appear exclusive and thereby alluring. Celibacy springing from faith will not waver in the face of temptation. Nor will it shake at the realization that "I" may not marry (or remarry) as quickly as "I" had hoped, or at all.

If celibacy were practiced on a wide scale, singles would be free to build relationships on more solid foundations such as the attractions of personality, shared convictions, and sense of humor. Less emphasis would be placed simply on the degree of a person's alleged or imagined sexual expertise. All of this would be in keeping, furthermore, with the biblical promise that the Spirit of Christ has come to set us free, free indeed, free to become who we truly are in the love and grace of God.

By this point I hope that you are informed, inspired, and ready to begin a singles ministry in your church, or to enhance the one with which you are presently working. In the final chapter of this book I want to discuss how and why I founded a singles ministry, to offer a few tips, and to showcase some of the outstanding ministries with single Black adults across the nation.

Chapter Five
STARTING A SINGLE ADULT MINISTRY

The decision to start a singles ministry in your church is a major decision, and a worthwhile one. A lot of effort will be required to get the program off the ground. Even more work will be needed to keep things going. Be prepared for anything. You will need a good bit of stamina. Most of all, rely on God to enable you in this most vital ministry.

Several years ago I decided that I wanted to see a singles ministry in my church because I saw a large portion of the congregation's membership in need. The needs were diverse, yet they were the same. A large group of unconnected individuals was in need of connection.

I too was part of that group of individuals. I knew first-hand what it felt like to be alone in a crowd. As a newcomer to the city I had made a few friends, but I did not feel totally at home in my new church setting. Sitting in a pew alone was a new experience for me—an experience of seclusion that I did not want to feel while in a church. After all, church is supposed to be home for us, not an uncomfortable way station. I sometimes felt a pang of envy, watching families come into the sanctuary and sit together. Just having someone you know sitting beside you seemed to mean so much.

Going home to an empty apartment after having experienced a spiritually uplifting worship service was also a letdown. I wanted to tell somebody about what I had experienced in worship. I did not want to shut myself up in my apartment for the rest of the day. What I really longed for was a group of my peers at church—people who were just like me. So, with a wing and a prayer, I approached the senior pastor of my congregation, Rev. Zan W. Holmes, with the idea that we should have our own singles ministry. "Sounds good," he said. "What is it?"

Ministry with single adults was just getting off the ground in the 1970s. By the early '80s, when I got started, such ministries were somewhat rare in Black churches. Luckily, Dr. Holmes was (and is) a man with a futuristic vision. He was also able to see what was before his eyes each Sunday morning in the congregation, a congregation that was 50 to 60 percent single adult. With Dr. Holmes' blessing, and with a handful of other interested singles, we went to work and began carving out the kind of program that I had felt in my heart was needed. Today, the single adult ministry at St. Luke "Community" United Methodist Church, with over one hundred participants, continues to thrive and to serve as a model of ministry with singles.

Starting from Scratch

Watching a flourishing ministry among single adults is a great joy. Helping such a ministry to happen is a lot of work. Though planning and development will vary from one situation to another, furthermore, there are some key steps that are helpful to bear in mind. In the following paragraphs I want to share with you the five steps I have used, and now recommend, in order to build a singles ministry from scratch.

1. Discuss the idea with the senior pastor. Ensure that he or she is in favor of such a ministry. You cannot and should not try to begin such a group without pastoral consent and support.

2. Begin to meet with a small group of singles. These should be people who are interested in the idea of having a singles ministry at the church, and who are willing to work to make the group a reality.

   This core group needs to be informed on the topic of single adults in general. Members of the group should research the topics of single adults, and of ministry to single adults, through magazine articles and books. (Please note the recommended readings at the conclusion of this book.) The group should also examine church records, in order to determine the number of singles within the potential ministry of this congregation. Note also that this should include some idea not only of the number of singles who are already attached to the congregation in some way, but also the number of those who live within the ministry area of the congregation. Singles ministries can be beautiful tools for evangelism.

3. A next step would be for the core group to produce a survey of the singles who are already part of the congregation. (I am including a copy of a survey that I have used for this purpose in the appendix, page 56.) Such a survey can be distributed by mail or by hand during a worship service. The survey should poll singles as to their

interest level in a singles ministry, and their willingness to attend meetings.

This survey should also be designed to find out what the church means to singles, and how they would like to serve if given the opportunity. In many instances the status of singlehood is a stigma. Single people are often excluded from church leadership. (Whether the exclusion is intentional or unintentional makes little difference.) A singles ministry can and should be a means of overcoming such indifference, and building the participation of singles into the full life of the congregation.

4. Compile all of the information (i.e., the numbers of single persons, their status and interests, etc.) and use this to create a formal presentation to the appropriate boards, agencies, and pastoral staff of your congregation. This information will enable you to document the need for a singles ministry in your church should there be opposition.

In my experience, it is probably wise to anticipate some opposition. Some opposition may come, for example, from married persons who aren't quite sure what the role and purpose of a singles ministry will be. The term *singles* conjures up in some minds a swinging, irresponsible lifestyle. In this case it will be incumbent upon you to convince such doubters that a ministry to single adults will be just the opposite.

5. Once the plan to develop the ministry is approved, allow the core group to plan an opening event. Announce this event from the pulpit, and have it endorsed by the senior pastor. The first event might be a meeting in the fellowship hall after services, or a brunch at a nearby restaurant, or a Bible study at someone's home.

Let's say, for example, that the first event will be a combined Bible study and potluck dinner at one of the single's homes. Schedule the event about four to six weeks in advance, to ensure that it is included on all church organizational calendars. This advance planning also gives time for the printing of flyers or even invitations for the singles of the church. On the two Sundays prior to the event, ask the senior pastor to endorse the plan for the singles group and for the upcoming event from the pulpit. In the week before the event, ask the core group to launch a calling campaign to personally contact all of the singles of the church and to invite them to come.

At the initial event, allow all those present to express their ideas, dreams, and visions for the singles ministry. This will give them their proper sense of ownership in the group right from the start. From these initial comments and conversations, you should have the raw material for moving forward with your own plans in your own context. In any event, whatever the long-range vision, don't wait long to plan another group event. A great deal of ministry with singles happens just by being together.

Do's and Don'ts

Along with these five steps for starting a ministry, I would also like to share some insights concerning how to keep the ministry healthy and growing. Ministry with single adults brings great joy to all if done well. There are, however, some pitfalls that you will want to avoid. Here are a few of the do's and don'ts that I have discovered over the years.

Do pray. Keep the power of prayer alive in the group and in the planning and upkeep of the group. Ask the entire congregation to pray for the success of the ministry.

Do try to get men involved in the group. Black men can and do benefit from the nurturing and care that stems from singles ministries. Many men, however, whether they are Black or white, are not joiners by nature. A good idea is to involve men on the planning team. As a rule, singles ministries are dominated by women. You will do well to break this rule in every way you can.

Do maintain a Christian purpose as your backbone and mainstay. The singles at St. Luke intended to keep the ministry of Christ at the center of their gathering, so they chose a special name to reflect this commitment. They decided to call themselves "S.O.L.E."—Singles of Life Everlasting. A vital element of any singles ministry is that it *is* a ministry. There are loads of social outlets for singles. The ministry of the church offers them the best in the world—Jesus Christ.

Do recruit aggressively. Don't be afraid to gently approach a single person in the congregation and offer an invitation to an event.

By the same token, there are a number of pitfalls that can get in the way of ministry with single adults. The following are some of the more common ones I have encountered. These are things you definitely do not want to do.

Don't be upset by a low turnout or by apathy. It takes some people a while to warm up to the idea of a program designed to meet their specific needs. In the Black community we are rarely catered to in this way. It's a real treat to have a customized ministry offered just for your group. Some people may not be ready for this.

Don't expect everyone to join. The idea of a singles ministry strikes some people as a group for losers. Also, many people today are overextended. They hold memberships in lots of groups and do not have the time for one more. Encourage such busy people to attend occasional events.

Don't judge the group's members on the basis of their careers. A person who works as a waiter may have the same if not more skills than a corporate manager. Remember that in our community we have not all had the same chance to make it. Much to my amazement, the stalwart of the group I started was a custodian. He was talented, creative, and a good leader.

Favorite Activities

In addition to the steps for getting started, and the "do's and don'ts" for growing as a group, every ministry with single adults will want to discover a list of favorite activities. Once again, and it almost goes without saying, every group will be different. Every group will want to discover its own favorite projects, outings, and places to go. Some activities are, however, time-honored and tested. Therefore, you might want to consider some of these in the short- and long-range planning for your group.

Bible study: An exciting opportunity for ministry and sharing is possible whenever two or more are gathered around the Word of God. Singles ministries should be biblically based. As it is with all Christians, so it is especially with singles: The strength and power needed to face and overcome the pressures of life can come through sharing God's Word.

Happy hours: Singles are looking for a place where they can truly "meet" one another. In secular culture, happy hour is supposed to be a way for singles to meet one another. Of course, in many secular clubs singles have to be willing to try to meet each other in a setting where the lights are dim, the music is blaring, and the chances of carrying on a "real" conversation in a nonthreatening way are, to say the least, slim. For these reasons, Christian happy hours are quickly becoming very popular.

The idea of a Christian happy hour, therefore, is something about which to be creative and to rejoice. Why not pick a special meeting place, one that is conducive to listening and to sharing? Or provide a place in the fellowship hall of your congregation's building. This should be a place where singles can come to listen to music—gospel jazz, light jazz, or gospel rap. Create an inviting atmosphere and serve punch as the beverage of choice. In doing so you can provide a place for singles to meet one another, to form faithful friendships and, yes, in some cases, even to discover a sense of true calling to the relationship of marriage. This too can be a source of great joy among a group of committed Christian singles.

Rap sessions: Another activity that generates interest and involvement is a rap session. Rap sessions are opportunities to discuss topics such as sex, dating, marriage, etc. Christian singles need opportunities to discuss such topics openly and honestly. Since the opportunity for such discussions is often scarce, you may find that rap sessions attract singles from other congregations, as well as from your own. Rap sessions may also attract singles in your own congregation who have been reluctant to get involved in other kinds of activities. This can be a good opportunity to spark their interest in the group.

Retreats/Outings: Everyone loves to get away from the normal routine for a while. For singles, however, getting away can be a lonely experience. To remedy this, some singles groups plan occasional outings—for example, weekend retreats at local campgrounds, retreat centers, or hotels. A retreat with singles can be centered around a variety of relevant themes, and led by a person trained in that field. Outings are also popular because many singles dislike attending public functions alone. Singles outings to movies, plays, and restaurants are crowd pleasers.

Successful Singles Ministries Across the Nation

I am certain that there are numerous exciting ministries with single adults all over the country. In preparing for this book, in fact, I have had the opportunity to talk with persons working in ministries located from coast to coast. They've shared what's going on in their ministries, and some of their secrets for success. Here are just a few of the successful ideas from five of the ministries that it has been my pleasure to witness.

Washington, D.C.—Metropolitan Baptist Church

According to leader Lisa Wilson, the key to success in this one hundred fifty-member singles group is being well-organized. "We have a core group of ten persons that keeps the program running smoothly and efficiently. We publicize all our events churchwide as well as citywide well in advance."

In my opinion, the most notable of this group's activities is its singles coffeehouse. A local singing group provides entertainment for a while. Then the singles set up tables and play board games such as Bible Trivia. At the end of their time together, the group closes with prayer.

Other highly successful events are seminars. In particular, Ms. Wilson mentioned a seminar built on an extremely popular topic: How to choose a marriage partner. "Marriage is so important because so many women want to be married," she said. "They've tried their way for so long. Now they are looking for answers from the Bible."

Charlotte, North Carolina—Friendship Baptist Church

With one hundred fifty to two hundred singles who are active in the singles ministry, the Rev. Bonnie Hines, associate pastor, has her hands full. She shared her answer to a common problem with singles ministries—a large turnout for social events and a small turnout for spiritually oriented events. To remedy this, the Rev. Hines and group leaders sponsored a combination pool party/Bible study. Only the Bible study portion of the event was a surprise. She stated that the event was a "success and everyone soon realized that Bible study could be fun."

Dallas, Texas—St. Luke "Community" United Methodist Church

Although I've already discussed much of the singles program at St. Luke, there is an important component to this ministry that I have not discussed, the single parents ministry. This group of about forty singles is dedicated to being a support network for each other with special reference to the needs found among singles who are also parents. "Basically what this group is all about is caring for each other," explained Jackie Moore, an active member of the group and now a special consultant to single parents.

"The group's activities included small things such as babysitting for one another, as well as large things such as setting up a big brother mentoring type of program for the parents that had young boys," she said. "Also a variety of events is planned for the parents only, as well as events for the parents and children together. Our rap sessions are especially popular due to the focus on topics such as how to relate to your ex-spouse in front of the children, child support, and how to get back into the dating scene," Ms. Moore added.

Currently this group has a monthly newsletter of its own and has taken on a mission project in the form of volunteering at a local shelter for homeless families.

Los Angeles, California—First African Methodist Episcopal Church

This unique ministry to singles has a decidedly "social" focus. Singles leader Chauncey Carter explained that because the entire church is immersed in Bible study, the singles ministry chose to focus on social events of fellowship and entertainment. Thus far the group of more than one hundred fifty members has taken part in two cruises and a trip to the Holy Land. "We want the church to be a place for us at all times, not just on Sunday," said Ms. Carter.

Atlanta, Georgia—Cascade United Methodist Church

Singles ministry director Diane Givens recalled the day she made her first announcement about the formation of a singles group. "This is *not* the Cascade Desperado Club or a dating service," she said. "That's not what we are about. The best thing about our group is that we have friendships with no pressure. This gives you the chance to meet someone without immediately figuring out how to drag them down the aisle."

The seventy-five members of this singles group are involved in a host of activities. An especially innovative project that pairs low-income, inner-city, third-grade boys with several of the single young adult men of the church is called "boys to men." "This program gives the boys a chance to interact with men, to talk about school, personal concerns, and even their heroes. Otherwise these young boys would have no male role models."

Concluding Words

Ministry to single adults in the Black church is not a project to be taken lightly. It requires that one be cognizant of the interrelatedness of being Black, Christian, and single. It demands research, commitment, sensitivity, energy, and love. And as leaders of such groups, the ministry asks much of your personal time and efforts. I am glad you have taken time to read this book, and I hope that what I have shared will enhance your leadership in some way.

If implemented with genuine care and solid planning, I believe singles ministries can help the church reclaim its position of leadership in the Black community. By no means am I suggesting that singles ministries are a cure-all for the multitude of ills in the Black community, but I am placing faith in the power of God to work through a group of dedicated people who want to make a difference in this world. Simple things, such as learning how to treat each other, make a big difference when the act is multiplied around the country.

The most crucial issue for singles, which I want to reemphasize in closing, is the imbalanced male-female ratio. As I discussed earlier, this imbalance probably means that some Black women will never marry. This is an important point to bear in mind as you seek to be a leader of ministry with this group. A sense of calm and confidence in the Lord must win over chaos and despair.

Overall, I have hope for the future of singles ministries in the Black church. Despite all of the obstacles, I still cling to the words that Jesus uttered long ago, "With God all things are possible."

Appendix:
FIRST CHURCH ANYWHERE
SINGLE ADULT SURVEY

(The following survey can be adapted in a variety of ways to serve the particular needs of your congregation. If you want to conduct a confidential survey, for example, you can simply remove the line related to "name." In any case you will want to encourage your singles to fill out the survey as candidly as possible.)

1. Name _____

2. Gender: Male _____   Female _____

3. Age range   20's ( )   30's ( )   40's ( )   50's ( )
               60's ( )   70's ( )   80's ( )

4. Single status:
      Divorced _____   Widowed _____   Always-single _____

5. Children: No _____   Yes _____   How many? _____   Ages _____

6. What is the greatest joy of being single?

7. What is the greatest problem with being single?

8. Does your church's singles ministry meet your needs? Explain.

9. What is more important in a potential mate: Christian beliefs, occupation, appearance, or personality? Why?

10. Is celibacy a realistic option for you? Why?

11. Please check or list activities below that interest you.

Bible Related	*Sports*	*Enrichment Services*
Bible Study _____	Bowling _____	Seminars _____
Sunday School _____	Bicycling _____	Retreats _____
Special Worship _____	Horseback Riding _____	Workshops _____
Other	Other	Other

Appendix: First Church Anywhere Single Adult Survey

Please check or list activities below that interest you:

Eating	*Arts and Crafts*	*Civic Activities*
Potlucks ____	Plays ____	Neighborhood Repair ____
Barbecues ____	Art Galleries ____	Visit Sick ____
Picnics ____	Model Building ____	Volunteer Work ____
Other	Other	Other

(Use your imagination to create a survey that is suited to the situation of your congregation and to the needs of your singles. Another excellent resource for helping people identify their areas of interest in congregational life and ministry is the *Time and Talent Inventory,* also available from Discipleship Resources.)

ENDNOTES

Chapter One
1. U.S. Bureau of the Census, *Current Population Reports,* Series P-20, No. 433, "Marital Status and Living Arrangements: March 1988" table 1, (Washington, D.C.: U.S. Government Printing Office, 1989).
2. William Strickland, "The Future of Black Men," *Essence,* Vol. 20, No. 7 (November 1989), p. 50.
3. Andrew J. Cherlin, *Marriage, Divorce and Remarriage* (Cambridge, Mass.: Harvard University Press, 1981), p. 98. See also Census, "Marital Status and Living Arrangements," table 1.
4. Ibid., table 1.
5. Robert Schoen and James R. Kluegel, "The Widening Gap in Black and White Marriage Rates: The Impact of Population Composition and Differential Marriage Propensities," *American Sociological Review,* Vol. 28 (December 1988), p. 896.
6. Robert Staples, *The World of Black Singles: Changing Patterns of Male/Female Relations* (Westport, Conn.: Greenwood Press, 1981), p. 24.
7. Ibid., p. 24.
8. Ibid., p. 35, table 2.
9. Ibid.
10. "Trial marriages ending in court," *The Dallas Morning News,* 9 June 1989, section A, p. 6.
11. Marian Wright Edelman, *Families in Peril: An Agenda for Social Change* (Cambridge, Mass.: Harvard University Press, 1987), p. 5.

Chapter Two
1. U.S. Bureau of the Census, *Statistical Abstract of the U.S.: 1989,* 109th ed., No. 83 (Washington, D.C.: U.S. Government Printing Office, 1989).
2. U.S. Bureau of the Census, *Current Population Reports,* Series P-20, No. 433, "Marital Status and Living Arrangements: March 1988," table 1 (Washington, D.C.: U.S. Government Printing Office, 1989).
3. "Charge to the Task Force on the Black Aged," *The Crisis,* No. 6 (June-July 1984), p. 24.
4. *A Portrait of Older Minorities,* American Association of Retired Persons (brochure).

Chapter Three
1. Julia and Nathan Hare, *The Endangered Black Family: Coping with the Unisexualization and Coming Extinction of the Black Race* (San Francisco, CA: Black Think Tank, 1984), p. 79.
2. Kenneth and Maime Clark, "Emotional Factors in Racial Identification and Reference in Negro Children," *Journal of Negro Education,* 1950, pp. 341-50; and Kenneth Moreland, "Racial Acceptance and Preference of Nursery School Children in a Southern City," *Merrill-Palmer Quarterly of Behavior and Development,* Vol. VIII, 1962, p. 279.

Chapter Four
1. Lisa Sowle Cahill, *Between the Sexes: Foundations for a Christian Ethics of Sexuality* (Philadelphia: Fortress Press, 1985), p. 29.

For Further Reading

Chapman, Audrey B. *Man Sharing, Dilemma or Choice.* New York: William Morrow and Company, Inc., 1986.

Greenwaldt, Karen. *Singles Care One for Another.* Nashville, Tennessee: Discipleship Resources, 1989.

Hare, Julia and Nathan. *Crisis in Black Sexual Politics.* San Francisco: Black Think Tank, 1984.

──────. *The Endangered Black Family: Coping with the Unisexualization and Coming Extinction of the Black Race.* San Francisco: Black Think Tank, 1984.

Landgraf, John R. *Singling: A New Way to Live the Single Life.* Westminster/John Knox Press, 1990.

Madhubuti, Haki R. *Black Men: Obsolete, Single, Dangerous? The African American Family in Transition.* Chicago: Third World Press, 1990.

Sample, Tex. *U.S. Lifestyles and Mainline Churches.* Westminster/John Knox Press, 1990.

Sims, Claudette Elaine. *Don't Weep for Me.* Houston, Texas: Impressions, 1985.